1 / 12

CR

ATLANTA
HAWKS

by Drew Silverman

Printed in the United States of America,
North Mankato, Minnesota
062011
092011

 THIS BOOK CONTAINS AT LEAST 10% RECYCLED MATERIALS.

Editor: Chrös McDougall
Copy Editor: Anna Comstock
Series design and cover production: Christa Schneider
Interior production: Carol Castro

Photo Credits: Gregory Smith/AP Images, cover, 39, 40, 43 (bottom); NBAE/ Getty Images, 1; AP Images, 4, 9, 10, 13, 14, 17, 18, 23, 24, 26, 42 (top and middle); J. Walter Green/AP Images, 7; Focus on Sport/Getty Images, 21, 43 (top); Andrew D. Bernstein/NBAE/Getty Images, 28; Charles Kelly/AP Images, 30, 32; Alan Mothner/AP Images, 34; John Bazemore/AP Images, 37, 47; Mark J. Terrill/AP Images, 44

Library of Congress Cataloging-in-Publication Data
Silverman, Drew, 1982-
  Atlanta Hawks / Drew Silverman.
     p. cm. -- (Inside the NBA)
  Includes index.
  ISBN 978-1-61783-149-2
  1. Atlanta Hawks (Basketball team)--History--Juvenile literature. I. Title.
  GV885.52.A7S55 2011
  796.323'6409758231--dc22
                          2011012354

TABLE OF CONTENTS

CHAPTER 1

A RIVALRY IS BORN

During the late 1950s and early 1960s, the St. Louis Hawks were one of the two most dominant teams in the National Basketball Association (NBA). The Boston Celtics were the other.

Both teams had several future Hall of Fame players on the court. And both teams had a future Hall of Famer as their coach. From the 1956–57 season through the 1960–61 season, no NBA teams won more games than the Hawks and the Celtics. In fact, the Hawks reached the NBA Finals in 1957, 1958, 1960, and 1961. Their opponent was the Celtics all four times.

Their 1957 meeting was an all-time classic. Game 1 went to double overtime. Game 3 and Game 6 were both decided by only two points. The Hawks evened the series at three games each when forward Cliff Hagan tipped in a shot at the buzzer to win Game 6.

St. Louis held a one-point lead in the final minute of Game 7. But Celtics rookie

St. Louis Hawks forward Bob Pettit (9) leaps to attempt a shot against the Cincinnati Royals in a 1957 game.

center Bill Russell blocked Jack Coleman's shot and scored on the other end to give Boston the late lead. The Celtics eventually won 125–123 in double overtime.

St. Louis star forward Bob Pettit missed a shot in the final seconds that would have tied the game. But overall, he had a successful postseason. He averaged a league-high 29.8 points in the playoffs. He also grabbed 16.8 rebounds per game in the postseason. Pettit was already known as a great NBA player. His signature moment came the following season.

Entering Game 6 of the 1958 NBA Finals, the Hawks led the Celtics three games to two. The Hawks were 48 minutes away from winning their first NBA championship. Pettit made sure the title would be theirs. He scored 50 points that night, including 19 of the Hawks' final 21 points. His tip-in with 15 seconds left secured the 110–109 win and the championship.

"It was the highlight of my career," Pettit said years later. "It was probably the greatest game I ever played. It just happened to be in the sixth game of the championship, and we were able to win by one. We were the happiest people in the world."

The Hawks were able to build great teams around Pettit during many of his 11 seasons. Hagan, a muscular forward, made five All-Star teams with the Hawks. Center/forward

The Hawks' Cliff Hagan (16) guards the Celtics' Bill Sharman during Game 2 of the 1958 NBA Finals. Hagan scored 37 points in the game.

Ed Macauley, guard Slater Martin, and center/forward Clyde Lovellette also starred on the great Hawks teams of the 1950s. Point guard Lenny Wilkens joined the team as a rookie in 1960. All were later elected to the Hall of Fame.

However, the common bond between all of the great teams was the 6-foot-9 Pettit. He was as dangerous from the outside as he was from the inside. He was surprisingly mobile and could dominate a game with his rebounding. But his scoring touch was what made him great.

"In his day," said legendary Celtics coach Red Auerbach, "Bob Pettit was the best power forward there was."

The Celtics and the Hawks met in the NBA Finals again

OVERCOMING OBSTACLES

Things were not always easy for Bob Pettit. He was cut from his high school basketball team as a freshman. He failed to make the team again as a sophomore. So Pettit practiced even harder. He shot baskets in his backyard for two or three hours every day.

Eventually he made his high school team as a junior. By his senior year, he was a star. Pettit then went on to play at Louisiana State University. He was an All-American forward as a junior and a senior there. "Basically, getting cut made me more determined," Pettit said. "Probably it was a good thing that I was not good to start with."

Following the 2010–11 season, Pettit ranked 32nd on the NBA's all-time scoring list with 20,880 career points. He was 15th on the all-time rebounding list with 12,849. The NBA honored Pettit as one of its 50 greatest players in 1996.

in 1960 and 1961. Boston won both times. Still, it was a period of great success for St. Louis. The Hawks finished first in their division four straight years from 1958 to 1961. After 1961, the team won its division a total of five times through 2010–11.

Pettit played for the Hawks—in Milwaukee and then in St. Louis—during his entire career, from 1954 to 1965. He was one of the NBA's first superstars. In 1954, the Milwaukee Hawks selected Pettit with the second pick in the NBA Draft. He was the NBA's Rookie of the Year in 1954–55. The Hawks moved to St. Louis for the next season. Pettit led the league in scoring and rebounding and was named the NBA's Most Valuable Player (MVP) that year. In 1958–59, he won the MVP Award for a second time.

Hawks forward Bob Pettit holds his 1958 All-Star Game MVP trophy. He was an All-Star in each of his 11 seasons and the MVP four times.

When he retired after the 1964–65 season, Pettit was the NBA's all-time leading scorer with 20,880 points. He also held the record for field goals made and minutes played, though Kareem Abdul-Jabbar eventually broke all of those records. For his career, Pettit averaged 26.4 points and 16.2 rebounds per game. He had his No. 9 jersey retired by the Hawks and was inducted to the Naismith Memorial Basketball Hall of Fame in 1971.

Many consider Pettit to be the greatest player in Hawks history. And his teams of the late 1950s and early 1960s are known as some of the best teams the Hawks have ever had.

CHAPTER 2

HAWKS BEGINNINGS

In 1946, the National Basketball League (NBL) awarded a franchise to Buffalo, New York. The team was called the Bisons. However, just 13 games into its first season, the team moved to Moline, Illinois. Team owner Ben Kerner then renamed it the Tri-Cities Blackhawks. The Tri-Cities included Moline, as well as Rock Island, Illinois, and Davenport, Iowa.

Three years later, the NBL merged with the Basketball Association of America to form the NBA. The Tri-Cities Blackhawks were one of the NBA's first 17 teams. They began play in the Western Division, where they finished in third place their first year in 1949–50.

In their second season, the Blackhawks finished last in the Western Division. Even worse, the team realized it could not make enough money in the Tri-Cities area. So, the team moved to Milwaukee, Wisconsin, in 1951 and shortened its nickname to the Hawks.

Hawks Hall of Fame guard Slater Martin goes up for a layup in a 1957 game. Martin played with the Hawks from 1956–57 to 1959–60.

Honoring the Past

When the team moved from Buffalo to the Tri-Cities in 1946, the nickname changed from the Bison to the Blackhawks. The new nickname was meant to honor the rich history of the Tri-Cities area. More than a century earlier, the Blackhawk War had taken place there. Chief Black Hawk, the leader of the Sauk Indians, had raised his tribe in Rock Island, Illinois—one of the Tri-Cities. So, the team became known as the Blackhawks.

The switch to Milwaukee was a good move financially, but the team did not have much success there. The Hawks went through three coaches during four seasons there, and finished last every year.

The Hawks' fortunes finally started to turn around in 1954, when they chose power forward Bob Pettit with the second pick in the draft. Pettit's 11-year run with the Hawks would produce many of the greatest moments in team history.

However, Pettit's Hall of Fame career with the Hawks started off with yet another change of cities. Prior to the 1955–56 season, the Hawks moved from Milwaukee to St. Louis, Missouri. Kerner moved the team, in part, because Milwaukee sports fans were focused on their new baseball team, the Braves.

St. Louis proved to be a great fit. Pettit was emerging as a star, and the team was becoming a contender. Then, on April 29, 1956, the Hawks and the Boston Celtics made a trade that changed the NBA forever.

The Hawks had the second pick in the draft that year. They chose Bill Russell, an imposing center from the University of San Francisco. The Celtics coveted Russell, while the Hawks were hesitant to pay the $25,000 signing bonus that he was asking for.

The Hawks began to turn around with the 1954 addition of forward Bob Pettit (9), who is shown defending against the Minneapolis Lakers.

So, the Hawks agreed to trade Russell to Boston in exchange for two players. The first was Ed Macauley, a 6-foot-8 center who was a six-time All-Star. More importantly, he had played at St. Louis University, and the team thought he could help draw fans to Hawks home games. The other player in the trade was rookie forward Cliff Hagan. He had also played nearby at the University of Kentucky.

Hawks forward Cliff Hagan goes for a hook shot over Boston Celtics defender Bill Russell, *left*, during the 1958 NBA Finals.

It seemed like a good trade for both teams, and to some extent it was. Macauley and Hagan helped the Hawks reach the NBA Finals four times and win the championship in 1958. But the trade turned the Celtics into a dynasty. With Russell leading the way, Boston won 11 championships from 1957 to 1969. Three of those titles came against the Hawks.

After the Russell trade, the Hawks still had plenty of good years in St. Louis. From 1956 to 1968, the Hawks only missed the playoffs once. They won six division titles during that stretch. And they reached the NBA Finals four times—the only four times in team history through 2010–11.

For a stretch in the late 1950s and early 1960s, the Hawks were the most profitable team in professional basketball. "Today I'm a national figure," Kerner said in 1960. "I could have been a national bum."

On the court, the Hawks sent nine different players to the All-Star Game during their 13 seasons in St. Louis. Pettit was the Hawks' superstar when they were in St. Louis. But he was hardly alone. St. Louis teammates Hagan, Macauley, center Clyde Lovellette, guard Slater Martin, and point guard Lenny Wilkens all joined him in the Hall of Fame.

After Pettit retired in 1965, the Hawks went through some rough years. In 1965–66,

COACHING CAROUSEL

The Hawks had 10 head coaches during their 13 years in St. Louis. Two of them went on to become Hall of Famers after Hawks' owner Ben Kerner fired them. Red Holzman coached the Hawks in 1955–56 and for the first 33 games of the 1956–57 season before Kerner fired him. Holzman later coached the New York Knicks to NBA titles in 1970 and 1973.

Alex Hannum coached the Hawks in their final 31 games of 1956–57 season. He returned the following year and led St. Louis to its only NBA championship. But that still was not good enough for Kerner. He replaced Hannum with Andy Phillip for the 1958–59 season. Phillip only lasted 10 games as Hawks coach. Meanwhile, Hannum went on to lead the Philadelphia 76ers to the NBA title in 1967. "I never liked Hannum," Kerner said. "I didn't feel safe with him. He wasn't loyal."

St. Louis finished third in the Western Division with a 36–44 record. By comparison, the team had won at least 40 games in seven of the previous eight seasons.

Led by Wilkens and center Zelmo Beaty, the Hawks rebounded to come in second place in 1966–67. However, they still lost more games than they won, finishing at 39–42. For the second straight year, St. Louis was eliminated in the second round of the playoffs. It marked the sixth straight season that the Hawks failed to win their division. But that streak ended in 1968.

With their 56–26 record, the Hawks won the Western Division by four games over the Los Angeles Lakers. Hawks coach Richie Guerin was named the NBA's Coach of the Year. But the excitement did not last long. The San Francisco Warriors upset the Hawks in the first round of the playoffs.

Even worse for the fans of St. Louis, news broke that the team was moving again. Kerner believed that the team could no longer compete financially in St. Louis. So, he sold the team to Georgia businessman Thomas Cousins and former Georgia governor Carl Sanders. The new owners moved the franchise to Atlanta, Georgia.

"[The Hawks] have been all my life, not just a part of it," Kerner said at the time of the

Hawks point guard Lenny Wilkens slips beneath a San Francisco Warriors defender before making a basket during the 1967 playoffs.

sale. "But the lack of attendance the past five years convinced me that the interest isn't there anymore."

CHAPTER 3

GOING SOUTH

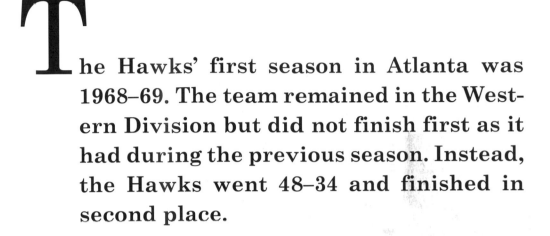

T he Hawks' first season in Atlanta was 1968–69. The team remained in the Western Division but did not finish first as it had during the previous season. Instead, the Hawks went 48–34 and finished in second place.

Prior to the season, the Hawks traded point guard Lenny Wilkens to the Seattle SuperSonics for veteran guard Walt Hazzard. That trade opened up minutes for Hawks third-year swingman Lou Hudson to become a star.

Hudson averaged 21.9 points, 6.6 rebounds, and 2.7 assists per game in 1968–69. That same year, he made his first of six consecutive All-Star teams.

With Hudson leading the charge, the Hawks finished first or second every year between

Hawks forward Lou Hudson goes for a layup during a 1967 game. He became a star soon after the Hawks moved to Atlanta in 1968–69.

Dr. J

In 1972, high-flying forward Julius Erving became eligible for the NBA Draft. At the time, he was playing for the Virginia Squires of the American Basketball Association (ABA). The Milwaukee Bucks chose Erving in the first round of the draft, but Erving instead chose to sign a contract with the Atlanta Hawks. Erving, known as "Dr. J," reported to the Hawks training camp and began practicing with the team. He played in three exhibition games with Atlanta. But then, a panel of judges ruled that Erving was legally obligated to return to the Squires. Erving eventually got to the NBA in 1976, but he never actually played for the Hawks.

1967 and 1974. However, they were unable to make any deep playoff runs during that period.

Part of the problem was the arrival of Pete Maravich, the team's first-round pick in the 1970 draft. Maravich, a 6-foot-5 shooting guard, was one of the greatest college players of all time. But his style did not mesh well in Atlanta. Maravich liked to do fancy dribbling and make flashy passes. He was a terrific scorer and playmaker, but his showboating style did not always lead to victories.

"Raw talent-wise, he's the greatest [player] who ever played," Hudson told *Sports Illustrated* in 1978. "The difference comes down to style. He will be a loser, always, no matter what he does. That's his legacy."

In fairness, Maravich did not have it easy. He was subjected to taunts from teammates who resented his enormous salary. And, some Hawks veterans were upset that Maravich was getting so much attention before he proved himself.

"A lot of guys who might have been good [would have] cracked under such circumstances," Wilkens said years later. "Pete kept his wits. He hung in there. He survived."

Pete Maravich was a star in college but struggled to fit in with the Hawks. He played in Atlanta from 1970–71 to 1973–74.

The Hawks had a winning record in just one of Maravich's four seasons in Atlanta. In 1973–74, Maravich attempted more shots than anyone in the league. But the team won just 35 of 82 games. At that point, the Hawks felt that it was time for Maravich to move on. They traded him to the New Orleans Jazz for two players and four draft picks. But then things went from bad to worse.

In the 1974–75 season, Hudson suffered an elbow injury and played in only 11 games all year as the Hawks dropped to a 31–51 record. Rookie forward John Drew helped pick up the slack, averaging 18.5 points and 10.7 rebounds per game. In Drew's second season, Atlanta fell apart down the stretch, losing 28 of its final 34 games.

The Hawks finished 29–53 that season. The next season they won 31 games. Meanwhile, Maravich was having some of his best NBA seasons. He led the league in scoring with the

In Demand

Four professional sports teams drafted Dave Winfield, who went on to become a Major League Baseball (MLB) Hall of Fame outfielder. The Hawks selected Winfield in the fifth round of the 1973 NBA Draft. The ABA's Utah Stars, MLB's San Diego Padres, and the National Football League's Minnesota Vikings also drafted Winfield, even though he never played college football. "He was the best athlete I'd seen in all my life," said Padres coach Don Williams.

Jazz in 1976–77 and went on to have a Hall of Fame career.

One bright spot for the Hawks during the 1970s was their international scouting. The Hawks became one of the first NBA teams to look for talented players in Europe and Asia. Under general managers Marty Blake and Stan Kasten, the team became known for its ability to judge international players.

Atlanta drafted Dino Meneghin from Italy in 1970. He was the first foreign player drafted by an NBA team. However, he stayed and starred in Italy, never making it to the NBA. Over the next 20 years, the Hawks would draft 10 more foreign players.

"We were pioneers," said Mike Fratello, who coached the Hawks from 1983 to 1990. "We had a general manager, Stan Kasten, who had really great

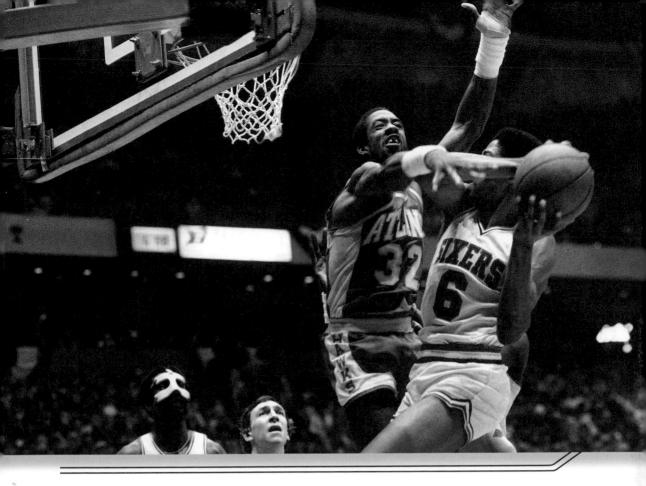

The Hawks' Dan Roundfield tries to stop Philadelphia 76ers star Julius Erving during a 1980 playoff game.

foresight. Stan was very perceptive in understanding that there was a lot of talent in other countries we needed to start paying attention to."

In January 1977, the Hawks made big news off the court. Ted Turner, owner of MLB's Atlanta Braves, announced that he had purchased the team. The Braves had also previously played in Milwaukee. Turner's acquisition of the Hawks brought the team more exposure. It also brought the franchise more stability. Turner promised that he would not move the team

Hawks guard Charlie Criss chases after a loose ball during the 1980 playoffs. He played for the Hawks in the late 1970s and early 1980s.

anymore. So after bouncing between four cities from 1946 to 1968, the Hawks finally had a permanent home in Atlanta.

The Hawks once again were showing signs of improvement. They continuously improved from 29 wins in 1975–76 until they reached 50 wins in the 1979–80 season. During those final four seasons, Hubie Brown was the Hawks' coach. He was known for getting the most out of his players and was named the NBA's Coach of the Year in 1977–78.

"We've proved that you don't need stars to win," said Frank Layden, the Hawks' director of player personnel at the time. But Brown wanted more.

"I want to prove that we're for real," he said in March 1979. "It would mean so much."

In 1979–80, the Hawks proved that they could once again win the Central Division title—their first since 1970. Brown's team featured a balanced scoring attack that year. Drew, guard Eddie Johnson, and forward/center Dan Roundfield all averaged between 16 and 20 points. However, all three players saw their scoring averages decline in the playoffs. The Philadelphia 76ers eliminated the Hawks, four games to one, in a second-round series.

The Hawks won their first four games of the 1980–81 season. But then they began a nightmare stretch in which they lost 13 of their next 14 games. Brown was fired before the season ended. The team finished in fourth place in the division at 31–51.

The following season, Turner hired Kevin Loughery to coach the Hawks. Loughery immediatcly led Atlanta to 11 more wins than it had the previous season. But the team still lost in the first round of the 1982 playoffs. Fortunately for the Hawks, though, help was on the way.

Moving Around

The Hawks are one of four NBA franchises that have been located in at least three different cities during their NBA history. The now Atlanta Hawks also played in Tri-Cities, Milwaukee, and St. Louis. The Kings played in Rochester, New York; Cincinnati, Ohio; and Kansas City, Missouri, before moving to Sacramento, California. They also played some games in Omaha, Nebraska, between 1972–75. The Clippers, who currently play in Los Angeles, also played in Buffalo, New York, and San Diego, California. And the Wizards franchise has been located in Chicago, Illinois; Baltimore, Maryland; and now Washington DC. No NBA franchise has ever played in more than four cities.

CHAPTER 4

THE "HUMAN HIGHLIGHT FILM"

I f the Bill Russell trade was the worst move in Hawks history, the Dominique Wilkins trade was the best move the team ever made. On September 3, 1982, the Hawks traded for the rookie from the University of Georgia. In return, they sent John Drew and Freeman Williams to the Utah Jazz. The trade changed the landscape of the team for more than a decade.

Wilkins went on to become the Hawks' all-time leading scorer. He scored 23,292 points for the Hawks, roughly 2,400 more than Bob Pettit. He retired as the seventh-highest scorer in NBA history with 26,668 career points. He was inducted into the

Ouch!

During a 1983 playoff game between the Hawks and the Celtics, Atlanta center Wayne "Tree" Rollins and Boston guard Danny Ainge got into a scuffle. At one point, Rollins bit Ainge's finger, forcing Ainge to get a few stitches. The next day, the Boston Herald ran the famous headline: "Tree Bites Man."

Hawks forward Dominique Wilkins became known for his monster slam dunks, such as this one against the Boston Celtics in a 1988 playoff game.

Hawks 5-foot-7 guard Spud Webb, *center*, poses with his much taller competition before the 1986 Slam Dunk Contest.

Hall of Fame in 2006. He also became known as "The Human Highlight Film" for his exciting plays and thrilling dunks.

But things did not start off smoothly for Wilkins. In his first three seasons, the Hawks averaged only 39 wins. They were knocked out in the first round of the playoffs in 1983 and 1984. In 1985, they did not even make the postseason. That off-season, during the summer of 1985, Wilkins had a change in attitude.

"I wanted to prove I was a total player. I wanted to change people's opinion of me," he said. "It bothered me that I had never made an All-Star team, that people thought all I could do was dunk."

So, Wilkins worked on his jump shot. He improved his passing skills and his rebounding. Most of all, he honed his leadership abilities.

That 1985–86 season, Wilkins made his first All-Star team. He led the league in scoring with 30.3 points per game, and he helped the Hawks to 50 victories. It was their first 50-win season since 1980. And the Hawks defeated the Detroit Pistons in the first round of the playoffs. It was the Hawks' first postseason series win since 1979.

In Game 2 of that series, Wilkins scored 50 points. That was the most anyone had scored in a playoff game since 1975. And, Wilkins scored those 50 points without making a single dunk.

"Boy, that's unbelievable, isn't it?" Wilkins said, shaking his head after the game.

SPUD WEBB

As much as anything in the 1980s, the Hawks were known for dunking. Dominique Wilkins won the NBA's second-ever Slam Dunk Contest in 1985. The following year, Wilkins finished second, but another Atlanta player took first place. That player was Anthony "Spud" Webb.

Wilkins and Webb were both great dunkers. The difference was that Wilkins was 6-foot-8, while Webb was only 5-foot-7. "I think it changed the way people looked at little guys," said Webb, the third-shortest player in NBA history through 2010–11. Webb played in the NBA from 1985 to 1998. Seven of those seasons came in Atlanta. Hawks coach Mike Fratello also stood just 5-foot-7. However, neither man was overwhelmed in a world of giants.

"I didn't listen to [the criticism]," Webb said. "If I listened to it, I would have been a season ticket holder."

Hawks center Moses Malone averaged 20.2 points per game in 1988–89, second only to Dominique Wilkins's 26.2 on the Hawks.

"No way this would've happened before this season."

The Boston Celtics beat the Hawks in the second round of the playoffs, but the season showed definite improvement. It continued in the following season. The Hawks won 57 games, claimed the Central Division title, and again reached the second round of the playoffs.

During that season, Wilkins's desire to beat Boston was greater than ever. "Nobody wants [to play] the Celtics worse than I do," he said. "The Celtics have had us for dinner quite a few times. It's time for things to change."

To Wilkins's disappointment, the Hawks did not face the Celtics in the 1987 playoffs. However, the teams did meet in the second round of the 1988 postseason. The series was a classic matchup of two great teams and two great superstars.

That season, Wilkins had averaged 30.7 points per game. It was the highest average of his career. Celtics star Larry Bird had averaged 29.9 points per game. The two were teammates in the All-Star Game, but they were enemies in the playoffs.

The Celtics won the first two games of their second-round series. The Hawks answered with three straight wins. But the Celtics won Game 6. That meant the series would come down to Game 7 in Boston.

That night, Wilkins and Bird went toe-to-toe in an epic showdown. Wilkins scored 47 points, including 16 in the fourth quarter. Bird scored 34 points, including 20 in the final 10 minutes. The Celtics won the game, 118–116.

"They each put their team on their back and said, 'Let's go,'" said Hawks coach Mike Fratello.

"A lot of games, you wonder what more you could have done," said Wilkins. "But not today. I can honestly say I did everything I could. We all did."

Still, the Hawks' season was over. Their run of success was beginning to fade, too. The Hawks won 52 games in 1988–89. But the team slowly began to slip after that.

Never again would the Hawks win a playoff series with Wilkins. They missed the playoffs entirely in 1989–90 and 1991–92. Wilkins suffered a foot injury in 1992, at which point his critics said his best basketball was behind him.

However, the Hawks organization continued to stand by its star player. "He just might be the youngest 33 [-year-old]

Dominique Wilkins starred for the Hawks for 11 1/2 seasons but was never able to carry the team past the second round of the playoffs.

in basketball," Hawks president Stan Kasten said.

The following season, in 1992–93, Wilkins eclipsed the 20,000-point mark for his career. He was the 17th player in NBA history to reach that milestone. But the Hawks were stuck in mediocrity. For the fourth straight season, they won between 38 and 43 games. In the playoffs, the Chicago Bulls swept them, three games to none, in the first round.

The Hawks brought the Wilkins era to an end the following February. Atlanta general manager Pete Babcock traded Wilkins to the Los Angeles Clippers for forward

Danny Manning. Both players were scheduled to become free agents that summer.

The positive for the Hawks, at the time, was that Manning was six years younger. And Manning was viewed as a smarter all-around player than Wilkins.

"Danny's smart, and I like that," said Lenny Wilkens, now the Hawks' coach. "You have to have that type of player on the floor if you're going to win, because you have to make good decisions down the stretch."

Babcock initially called the match "a perfect fit," but it wasn't. Manning only played in 26 regular-season games and 11 playoff games for the Hawks before signing with the Phoenix Suns as a free agent. Meanwhile, Wilkins spent his final three NBA seasons with the Boston Celtics, the San Antonio Spurs, and the Orlando Magic.

He never made another All-Star team.

Still, despite what his critics said, Wilkins brought many great memories to a generation of Hawks fans. "Dominique is a showman. . . . 'Nique works so hard. He loves the game, and he never takes a night off," Kasten said. "People always talk about what he doesn't do. But what more could you ask than what he does?"

Dreamin'

Dominique Wilkins never hid his disappointment over not being selected for the 1992 US Olympic Team. Known as the Dream Team, many consider the 1992 squad to be the greatest basketball team ever assembled. "It bothers me, sure it does," he said several months after the Dream Team won the gold medal in Barcelona, Spain. "I'd never say anybody shouldn't have been there, but I think I could've been on the team, too. I don't think, all in all, I've gotten respect over the years. I really don't know why. Maybe it's because we haven't won it all."

CHAPTER 5

THE NEW ERA

Through 2010–11, the Hawks had not won a division title or made it past the second round of the playoffs since trading Dominique Wilkins in 1994. However, Atlanta has had plenty of good players and good teams since Wilkins left. And plenty of good coaches, too.

The Hawks won at least 50 games in both 1996–97 and 1997–98. Each of those seasons came under the guidance of former Hawks star Lenny Wilkens, who coached the team from 1993 to 2000. He left Atlanta as the winningest coach in NBA history, but he never could lead the Hawks to playoff glory.

Atlanta's best team under Wilkens was the 1996–97 squad. That team won 56 games, led by 7-foot-2 center Dikembe Mutombo. He had signed as a

Center Dikembe Mutombo was one of the most intimidating defenders in the NBA during his 4 1/2 years with the Hawks, beginning in 1996–97.

THE STOPPER

Dikembe Mutombo grew up in the African nation of Congo. He became one of the NBA's top rebounders and shot blockers soon after the Denver Nuggets selected him fourth overall in the 1991 draft.

Mutombo played for the Hawks from 1996–97 until midway through the 2000–01 season. He was named the NBA's Defensive Player of the Year in 1997 and again in 1998. He made the All-Star team four times in his five seasons with the Hawks. And he became a fan favorite in Atlanta for wagging his finger at opponents after he blocked their shots.

Mutombo was also known for his generosity off the court. He founded the Dikembe Mutombo Foundation to aid poor, disadvantaged people in Africa. He also donated more than $3 million for construction of a new hospital in Africa. In 2000, Mutombo received a President's Volunteer Service Award for his generosity.

free agent prior to the season, and he proved to be one of the NBA's top defensive players.

The Hawks' 56–26 record was their best in a decade. Mutombo finished second in the league in rebounding and blocks. Point guard Mookie Blaylock led the NBA in steals per game. Shooting guard Steve Smith led the team in scoring at 20.1 points per game.

The Hawks went 36–5 at home that year. That tied the team record for most home wins in one season. However, the home record did not stand up in the playoffs. After beating the Detroit Pistons in the first round, the Hawks lost both of their home games to the Chicago Bulls in the second round. The Bulls won the series, four games to one.

The 1997–98 team went 50–32. Mutombo and Smith

Point guard Mookie Blaylock led the NBA with 212 steals in 1996–97. He played for the Hawks from 1992–93 to 1998–99.

both made the All-Star team, while Blaylock led the league in steals again. The strong regular season prompted forward Tyrone Corbin to state: "This team has all the pieces in place to win it all." But the playoffs proved to be another disappointment. They lost to the Charlotte Hornets in the first round.

The following season featured a 50-game schedule due to a lockout that stretched into the regular season. However, the Hawks enjoyed success during the shortened season. They went 31–19 and set the NBA record for fewest points allowed per game (83.4). But in the playoffs, the New York Knicks swept the Hawks four games to none in the second round.

"[The Knicks] came out and played well; we didn't and we're going home," Smith said.

The disappointment was only just beginning for the Hawks. The 1999–2000 season began a string of nine consecutive losing seasons. The team would not make the playoffs again until 2008. They wouldn't win another playoff series until 2009.

From a personnel standpoint, the new century featured one mistake after another. In 2001, the Hawks traded Mutombo to the Philadelphia 76ers for four players. Mutombo helped the 76ers reach the NBA Finals that season. The players the Hawks received never led Atlanta to the playoffs.

Over the next several seasons, the Hawks added more talented players, hoping for better results. They acquired forward Shareef Abdur-Rahim in a trade with the Vancouver Grizzlies in 2001. The next year, they got forward Glenn Robinson in a trade with the Milwaukee Bucks. During the 2003–04 season, the team traded for forward Rasheed

Guard Joe Johnson led the Hawks in scoring every season from 2005–06 through 2010–11. His 25 points per game in 2006–07 were a career high.

Wallace and then dealt him away 10 days later. Then, they brought in forward Antoine Walker for the 2004–05 season. Despite those players' past successes, none of the moves worked out particularly well.

The Hawks also faced tragedy in 2005, when backup center Jason Collier collapsed and died during the off-season. An autopsy found that Collier had an abnormally large heart, which caused a rhythm disturbance. He was just 28 years old.

Things finally began to look up for Atlanta in 2005–06. The team had just traded for swingman Joe Johnson. The move proved to be a steal. Johnson

Forward Josh Smith became known for his athletic dunks soon after entering the league with the Hawks in 2004–05.

helped the Hawks double their wins from 13 to 26 in his first season.

The Hawks' improved to 30 wins in 2006–07. Then, in 2007–08, they returned to the playoffs with a 37–45 record. Johnson made the All-Star team for a second straight season. The team also picked up veteran point guard Mike Bibby at the trade deadline, hoping he would help Josh Smith, who was emerging as one of the NBA's most athletic forwards.

The Hawks lost to the Celtics, the eventual NBA champions, in the first round of the playoffs in 2008. But they broke through in 2009. They finished second in their division with 47 wins—their most since

1997–98. Then they beat the Miami Heat in the first round of the playoffs before falling to the Cleveland Cavaliers in round two.

The 2009–10 season would follow a similar script. The Hawks again finished second in the division with 53 wins. But a second-round playoff loss to the Orlando Magic left much to be desired.

Atlanta won 44 games and returned to the playoffs as the fifth seed in 2010–11. The Hawks upset the Magic, four games to two, in the first round. Then they surprised the top-seeded Chicago Bulls with a 103–95 victory to start the second round. But behind NBA MVP Derrick Rose, the Bulls eventually won in six games.

Still, the Hawks have a promising core. Johnson is still regarded as one of the best shooting guards in the NBA.

Smith, Marvin Williams, and Al Horford give Atlanta a trio of talented young forwards.

Through 2010–11, the Hawks have not made it past the second round of the playoffs since moving to Atlanta. And they still have not won the championship since 1958. But there is reason to believe better days lay ahead.

Joe Johnson

Some Hawks fans were concerned when the Hawks traded a promising young player and two first-round draft picks for relatively unproven guard Joe Johnson during the summer of 2005. As it turned out, the trade was a solid one for the Hawks. In his first season with Atlanta, Johnson led the team in scoring, assists, steals, games played, minutes played, and three-point percentage. He made the All-Star team in four of his first five seasons with Atlanta. Yet, in a Sports Illustrated poll published in January 2010, Johnson was named the league's most underrated player.

TIMELINE

1946	The Tri-Cities Blackhawks begin playing in the NBL.
1951	The Blackhawks move to Milwaukee and become the Hawks.
1954	The Hawks draft Bob Pettit, a forward from Louisiana State, with the second pick in the draft. He becomes one of the greatest players in NBA history.
1955	The Hawks move from Milwaukee to St. Louis.
1956	The Hawks draft center Bill Russell from San Francisco and then trade him to the Boston Celtics. Russell goes on to a hall-of-fame career with the Celtics.
1957	The Hawks make the NBA Finals for the first time, losing to the Celtics.
1958	Behind Pettit's 50 points in the deciding Game 6, the Hawks defeat the Celtics to win the NBA title.
1960	The Hawks lose to the Celtics in the NBA Finals.
1961	The Hawks again lose to the Celtics in the NBA Finals.
1965	Pettit retires as the NBA's all-time leading scorer after 11 seasons.

1968	The Hawks move from St. Louis to Atlanta.
1970	The Hawks draft guard Pete Maravich from Louisiana State. He was one of the best college players ever but struggles in the NBA.
1974	The Hawks trade Pete Maravich to the New Orleans Jazz.
1982	The Hawks acquire rookie forward Dominique Wilkins from the Utah Jazz.
1986	Wilkins leads the NBA in scoring for the only time in his career.
1994	The Hawks trade Wilkins to the Los Angeles Clippers.
1995	Hawks coach Lenny Wilkens becomes the winningest coach in NBA history.
1999	During a strike-shortened season, the Hawks set the NBA record for fewest points per game allowed with 83.4.
2008	The Hawks return to the playoffs following an eight-year drought.
2011	The Hawks reach the second round of the Eastern Conference playoffs for the third straight year, but for the third straight year they are eliminated.

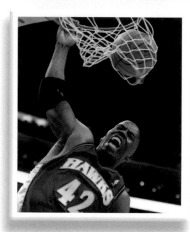

Cliff Hagan (G/F; 1956–66)
Lou Hudson (F/G; 1966–77)
Joe Johnson (G/F; 2005–)
Pete Maravich (G; 1970–74)
Dikembe Mutombo (C; 1996–2001)
Bob Pettit (F; 1954–65)
Doc Rivers (G; 1983–91)
Tree Rollins (C; 1977–88)
Josh Smith (F; 2004–)
Lenny Wilkens (G; 1960–68)
Dominique Wilkins (F; 1982–94)
Kevin Willis (F/C; 1984–94; 2004–05)

FRANCHISE HISTORY

Tri-Cities Blackhawks (1949–51)
Milwaukee Hawks (1952–55)
St. Louis Hawks (1955–68)
Atlanta Hawks (1968–)

NBA FINALS
(1949–, wins in bold)

1957, **1958**, 1960, 1961

DIVISION CHAMPIONSHIPS

1957, 1958, 1959, 1960, 1961, 1968,
1970, 1980, 1987, 1994

KEY PLAYERS
(position[s]; years with team)

Zelmo Beaty (C; 1962–69)
Mookie Blaylock (G; 1992–99)
John Drew (G/F; 1974–82)

KEY COACHES

Mike Fratello (1980–90):
    324–253; 18–22 (postseason)
Richie Guerin (1964–72):
    327–291; 26–34 (postseason)
Lenny Wilkens (1993–2000):
    310–232; 17–30 (postseason)

HOME ARENAS

Wharton Field House (1949–51)
Milwaukee Arena (1951–55)
Kiel Auditorium (1955–68)
Alexander Memorial Coliseum
    (1968–72)
Omni Coliseum (1972–97)
Georgia Dome (1997–99)
Philips Arena (1999–)

* All statistics through 2010–11 season

QUOTES AND ANECDOTES

The 1948–49 Tri-Cities Blackhawks featured the only 7-footer in the National Basketball League. His name was Don Otten, and he averaged a league-best 14 points per game.

At age 15, Dominique Wilkins used to challenge men in their twenties to one-on-one basketball games for $1. After he defeated the older guys, he would give the money to his mother to buy food. "I always thought he was working odd jobs, raking grass," his mother, Gertrude, told *People Weekly* years later. "She thought I was stealing it," Wilkins joked. "She was always second-guessing me."

When the Hawks won the 1958 NBA championship, they became the last all-white team to ever win the title. Technically, the Hawks did have an African-American player (Worthy Patterson). But he only played 13 minutes during the regular season and did not see action for the Hawks during the postseason.

Hawks coach Alex Hannum used to walk into the room where the players' wives waited after a game. He would turn to the women and ask, "Okay, who's mad at me because I'm not playing your husband?"

"Records are made to be broken, but this one lasted 28 years, which is an indication that breaking it was not an easy thing to do. If anybody had to do it, I'm glad Lenny did it." —Legendary Boston Celtics coach Red Auerbach on Hawks coach Lenny Wilkens, who surpassed Auerbach as the NBA's all-time winningest coach with a win over the Washington Bullets on January 6, 1995.

GLOSSARY

assist

A pass that leads directly to a made basket.

backcourt

The point guards and shooting guards on a basketball team.

contender

A team that is in the race for a championship or playoff berth.

draft

A system used by professional sports leagues to select new players in order to spread incoming talent among all teams. The NBA Draft is held each June.

dynasty

A team that dominates a particular league or sport for a period of time.

franchise

An entire sports organization, including the players, coaches, and staff.

free agent

A player whose contract has expired and who is able to sign with a team of his choice.

general manager

The executive who is in charge of the team's overall operation. He or she hires and fires coaches, drafts players, and signs free agents.

lockout

When an employer prevents employees from working, usually due to a labor dispute.

postseason

The games in which the best teams play after the regular-season schedule has been completed.

scouting

The search for talented players for a team to add.

swingman

A player who can play both guard and forward.

FOR MORE INFORMATION

Further Reading

Ballard, Chris. *The Art of a Beautiful Game: The Thinking Fan's Tour of the NBA*. New York: Simon & Schuster, 2009.

Marecek, Greg. *The St. Louis Hawks: A Gallery of Images and Memorabilia*. St. Louis: Reedy Press, 2007.

Pettit, Bob. *Bob Pettit: The Drive Within Me*. Englewood Cliffs, NJ: Prentice-Hall, 1966.

Web Links

To learn more about the Atlanta Hawks, visit ABDO Publishing Company online at **www.abdopublishing.com**. Web sites about the Hawks are featured on our Book Links page. These links are routinely monitored and updated to provide the most current information available.

Places to Visit

Missouri History Museum
5700 Lindell
St. Louis, MO 63112
314-746-4599
www.mohistory.org
This museum provides many exhibits on the history of Missouri life, including current and former sports teams such as the St. Louis Hawks.

Naismith Memorial Basketball Hall of Fame
1000 West Columbus Ave.
Springfield, MA 01105
413-781-6500
www.hoophall.com
This hall of fame and museum highlights the greatest players and moments in the history of basketball. Bob Pettit and Dominique Wilkins are among the former Hawks enshrined here.

Philips Arena
1 Philips Dr.
Atlanta, GA 30303
404-878-3000
www.philipsarena.com
This has been the Hawks' home arena since 1999. Tours are available when the Hawks are not playing.

INDEX

About the Author

Drew Silverman is a sports writer based in Philadelphia, Pennsylvania. He graduated from Syracuse University in 2004. He then worked as a sportswriter and editor at ESPN's headquarters in Bristol, Connecticut, before returning home to Philadelphia. After several years as sports editor for *The Bulletin* newspaper, he began working for Comcast SportsNet as a content manager. Silverman has covered everything from college basketball to Major League Baseball and National Football League games to the Stanley Cup Finals.